Werner Bischof
After the War

Werner Bischof
After the War

Foreword by Miriam Mafai

Smithsonian Institution Press
Washington, D.C.

Published 1997 in the United States of America
by Smithsonian Institution Press
in association with Federico Motta Editore, Milan

Library of Congress Cataloging-in-Publication Data

Bischof, Werner Adalbert, 1916–1954
    [Dopo la guerra. English]
    After the war / Werner Bischof; translated by Robert
Lockhart]
        p.   cm.
    Originally published in Italian in 1995 by Federico
Motta Editore of Milan
    ISBN 1-56098-721-9 (alk. paper)
    1. World War, 1939–1945—Destruction and pillage —
Europe—Pictorial works.   2. Reconstruction
(1939–1951)—Europe—Pictorial works. I. Title.
    D810.D6B55   1997
        97-1269   940.53—dc21

04 03 02 01 00 99 98 97   5 4 3 2 1

Printed by Arti Grafiche Motta, Milan
Manufactured in Italy, not at government expense

Foreword

Miriam Mafai

May 1995 marked fifty years since the end of the Second World War in Europe. In all the capital cities, military parades commemorated the occasion with great solemnity. An increasingly sophisticated display of weaponry, convoys of armored vehicles on the ground and warplanes in the sky swept past heads of state and government officials. In those homages to the military, war was celebrated rather than peace, and civilians were forgotten. But the civilians—and perhaps the civilians above all—were the protagonists of the war. Protagonists, not just victims.

In contrast to the First World War, the second—except for relatively brief periods—was not fought in trenches along static frontlines. It was instead a war of mobility, invasions, deportations, exterminations of entire populations. The first was a conflict among nations; the second, from the very beginning, assumed the character of a conflict between ideologies. Whereas military strategists and armies were the main actors in the First World War, in the second civilians fought alongside soldiers. It was a war fought behind the frontlines, often characterized by clandestine struggles against occupying forces, and thus by acts of terrorism and their reprisals, and, more, by bombings and hunger. Not only men who had been called to arms took part, but also the elderly, adolescents, women, and children. Citizens who were not just victims, but also participants—this was the most distinguishing feature of the Second World War.

The conclusion of the war, then, cannot be represented by the soldier returning home, the symbolic image of 1918. It is this, but not only this. What marks the end of the Second World War is a sort of deep breath rising from the ruins of Europe, the result of surprise, relief, and hope. It is the breath of survivors, of those who escaped the massacre and who sought to begin living again. I myself heard this breath, in May 1945. Werner Bischof also heard it, understood it, and miraculously captured it on film.

It was the summer of 1945 when the young photographer—who hadn't yet reached thirty—decided to begin his journey across a Europe destroyed by the war. Such a journey would have been nothing extraordinary if Bischof were a professional photojournalist, a lover of adventure (such as those who are delivered to us by the image of journalism in the movies). But Bischof, who had already achieved critical success in his work, was known instead as an erudite, refined creator of images on the edge of abstraction. Thus Manuel Gasser presented one of Bischof's portfolios in 1946: "These 24 photographs that Werner Bischof offers to those who love beautiful things are not only the product of his art but, at the same time, a conclusion and a farewell. The man who for hours upon hours polished and smoothed a snail and a conch shell to attain the desired brilliance of whiteness, the man expert in the most subtle devices for manipulating light and shade, the man who explored the most delicate objects as only a poet and dreamer could, one day this man put aside all that he had created and achieved, climbed into a jeep, and journeyed into the world devastated and disfigured by war: in Germany, in Holland, in Northern Italy. He set off to photograph."

The images gathered in this volume bear witness to Bischof's travels across Germany, France, Hungary, Holland, Greece, and Italy—countries victorious and vanquished. One initial observation: a majority of the time, Bischof's eye focuses and dwells on people more than objects. The ruins of war, those Coliseums of our time, certainly have their own tragic allure in the photographer's eye. But it is the faces of women and their children—protagonists and survivors of the war—which interest him most and on which he lingers in order to capture, in the instant between a fixed gaze and the hint of a smile, that breath of which I spoke—the surprise, relief, and desire to live.

This collection of photos opens with a spectral image of the destroyed Reichstag, a telling symbol of the defeat of Nazism and its mad hunger for power, and ends with Milan's Piazza Duomo, teeming with a crowd that could have gathered either for a political protest or, possibly, for nothing—a crowd convened without any other purpose than to enjoy a sunny Sunday afternoon. Indeed, peace makes both alternatives possible. The war had been over for a year, and all of Milan's great buildings—the Galleria, La Scala, San Babila, the Marino Palace—still bore visible marks of intense shelling. But life was returning, and the police officer once again took up his post to direct traffic.

Men, women, and children all began living again, and Bischof catches them in this delicate passage from war to peace, engulfed in a world that the fighting had turned into a heap of ruins. From a stone skeleton—possibly a church whose roof has been torn off by a bomb—two German girls skip, light-footed and smiling. Against the backdrop of what were once houses (how many people perished in that attack?), a group of children in Fribourg play ring-around-the-rosie, slender legs bare against the elements, hands stretched out to the their playmates.

Only a few years before, Europe was a land where war razed everything in its path, killing and destroying indiscriminately. Yet a glimmer of hope radiates from Bischof's photographs: The survivor who advances haltingly through a landscape of death, a basket hanging heavily from his arm, will find food; the woman carrying stones will find some clear spot to lay them down and begin rebuilding her home; the two German girls and the children of Freiburg no longer risk death by deportation, injuries, or hunger. I enjoy thinking that they are adults now, living in tranquil homes with children and grandchildren to whom they recount their stories of survival and teach a love of peace and fraternity among people of different nations, cultures, and religions. And I ask myself: what has become of the small boy with the round, dark eyes—innocent like those of a startled bird—who takes refuge in the arms of his grandmother, her graying hair covered with a dark kerchief folded in the tradition of Sardinian women, both their expressions desperately asking for meaning in the evils of the world? The sequence of those photographs is perfectly interrupted by a young girl who is captured in a moment of unguarded laughter as she carries water jugs across some rocky Sardinian beach—a serene image, and almost one of joy.

At the end of 1946, Werner Bischof made his way to Greece by obtaining an assignment with the Swiss relief organization Schweizer Spende, which was preparing emergency temporary housing for orphaned children at Ziros. The site is miserable, the living conditions are horrendous, and the most of laborers are in various states of shell shock. From there, though, he moves on to Athens and, on a clear sunny morning, ascends the Acropolis to take a few photos that seem to harken back to his traditional style. After the squalor at Ziros, Bischof's surrender to the beauty of the Caryatides seems to him almost a crime, and he attempts to justify it when he writes in his diary: "Unsatisfying work done only to get my bread, but the Americans will gladly take them. . . . People do like them."

From Greece, Bischof travels to Hungary, Romania, Czechoslovakia, and Poland. He does not speak the language and cannot travel easily freely because of the communication barrier as well as the authorities' suspicion toward such a peculiar traveler—a young Swiss photographer who, to say it in Bischof's own words, does not want to travel the countryside as an express train does, but rather to stop at each station—even the most remote—to look, reflect, and understand. In Eastern Europe, life is also beginning again, however laboriously, and he captures farmers moving their belongings to safety, a horse-drawn cart, a group of women waiting for the train (but from where and to where?), a monument—absurd in its grandiosity—rising into emptiness. Here also perceives with great unease the signs of profound political changes in progress. "We are very far from peace," he notes in his diary. An extraordinary premonition, given that Europe was already on the brink of entering the so-called Cold War. (But Bischof will protest a December 1949 *Life* photo essay, in which eleven pages of his photographs of Eastern Europe appear under the title "Countries Behind the Iron Curtain," accompanied by text on the Cold War.)

From Budapest, where he spends Christmas alone in 1947, Bischof would write to his father, "You don't understand, Father, that I am making this journey not to fulfill a desire for new experiences but to experience a complete transformation in my humanity. You say now would be a good time to return and take up more stable work. But Father, I can no longer take pictures of pretty shoes." The "complete transformation" was in progress. In postwar Europe, there were no more "pretty shoes" to photograph (or, more precisely, there were a few but they did not interest him in the least.) At that point in his life, it would have been quite easy, even justifiable, for Bischof to fall prey to the facile rationalization of desperation and despair. It would have been very easy indeed, above all because just a few years before he had been a master at capturing precise beauty in his photographs. But Bischof shuns the aesthetic and ideological temptation to return to the abstract and succeeds in capturing, in the complex events that unfolded before his eyes, the optimism and trust in the future and the simple desire to live that radiates from the Sardinian girl who carries her water jugs, from the electrician bent over his wires, from the peasant poised at the doorway of her cottage, from the child who playfully raises her dress near the drinking fountain, even from a loaf of bread and a basket of eggs arranged on a windowsill.

Such was Europe after the war. A continent that mourned its dead and, at the same time, began to rebuild homes and lives, immersed in despair and cautious optimism, possessed of a tenacious will to remember the evil and a desire to forget it altogether. We will remember our continent that way, those of us who lived during those years (those of us who had the fortune to have known it during those years). Through the sheer force of his intelligence and passion, Bischof returns it to us intact in these pages. On the occasion of the fiftieth anniversary of the end of the war, it is thus fitting to republish these of Bischof's photographs that celebrate the inexhaustible desire to live of men, of women, of children, of all those who suffered through the war, victors and vanquished.

Translated from the Italian by Robert Lockhart

Passages from the Diary of Werner Bischof
(chosen by his son Marco)

"Then came the war, and with it the destruction of my ivory tower. The suffering man's face became my central point of focus. I was working as a correspondent on the border between Switzerland and Austria, and there I saw thousands of wretched souls waiting for days behind the barbed wire—children and the elderly—with the explosion of grenades and the furious clanging of armored vehicles in the background. This sight pushed me toward understanding the true face of the world. Our peaceful, easy lives deprive us of the capacity to see the immense need outside of our immediate boundaries. Many gladly give their own contributions to relief work, but just enough to feel relieved from any spiritual conflict."

"After my first trip to Holland, France, and Luxemburg, the journal *Du* published my impressions, but what an indignant reaction! The cover image showing the face of an injured child upset people, who wanted only to preserve their own tranquility. At home I contemplated with dejection those tender images shot before the war, which had received so much praise, but in my mind I continued to picture hundreds of wretched people, whose spirits were crushed by constant grief and who needed our help."—St. Margrethen, Switzerland, 1944

"Bomb craters filled with water are ubiquitous all over Europe, and everything is in ruins. The train station is burned out, trains and trucks marked "Allied Forces" pass by a completely destroyed police station, clouds of gray-red and black fumes rise from a pile of rubble. This is my first view of total destruction. In the middle of a burned-out church I spy a tangle of rusted metal, which turns out to be objects of everyday use—a typewriter, cupboards, and bed frames. For me, who has never quite been able to develop an exact picture of reality, this was a disturbing experience. Then a woman comes out of cavern of rubble. "Are you hungry, do you want some of our food?" I follow her, not because I am hungry but because I want to see how people could live in these ruins. In a half-destroyed room, amid mud and walls soaked by rain, there are two beds, a hot plate, and infinite courage to begin life over again."—Freiburg, 1945

"Roermond is the last stop for today. A brief tour of the city, a tower gravely damaged. A blown-up bridge and next to it the piers of a new one as well as a provisional one made with boats lashed side by side. . . . The streets are crowded, and I often encounter children with guns and helmets for toys.

At the post office, where I am waiting, a young man arrives with a lacerated face: the blue-violet cauterization of the stitches, the glass eye, a blood-red mask of bandages, and the florid pink of raw meat form a horrible contrast. I give him a pack of Ovaltine."—Roermond, Holland, 1945

"I did not want to travel the countryside as an express train, so to speak, listening to other people's impressions, collecting prepared reports from various press offices, and, back at home, putting together abstracts with few personal observations. These days that type of journalism is too widespread, as it saves time and money. To this, one should also add that which is "lost" (which naturally refers to what the reader enjoys most of all.) For this reason, these correspondents have become modern narrators of fables. Because of these concerns and my increasing discomfort in feeling like I am "shut in a cage," I have pushed myself to seek a personal experience. I have not not given myself deadlines. It seemed to me better to first draw all the essentials from the abundance and then move on. Certainly there were governments that did not demonstrate a keen interest in a trip of this type and that refused to prolong my visa. Collaborating with the Schweizer Spende, I was able to develop an idea of the lives of those living in the countries of the East and can say that it was a positive experience for both sides."

"On one side lies the East—on the other the West. Both powers have serious problems of various kinds. If I succeed in representing this in and with children, I will have achieved a purely social, and at the same time European, work of art."—Eastern Europe, 1947–48

Photographs

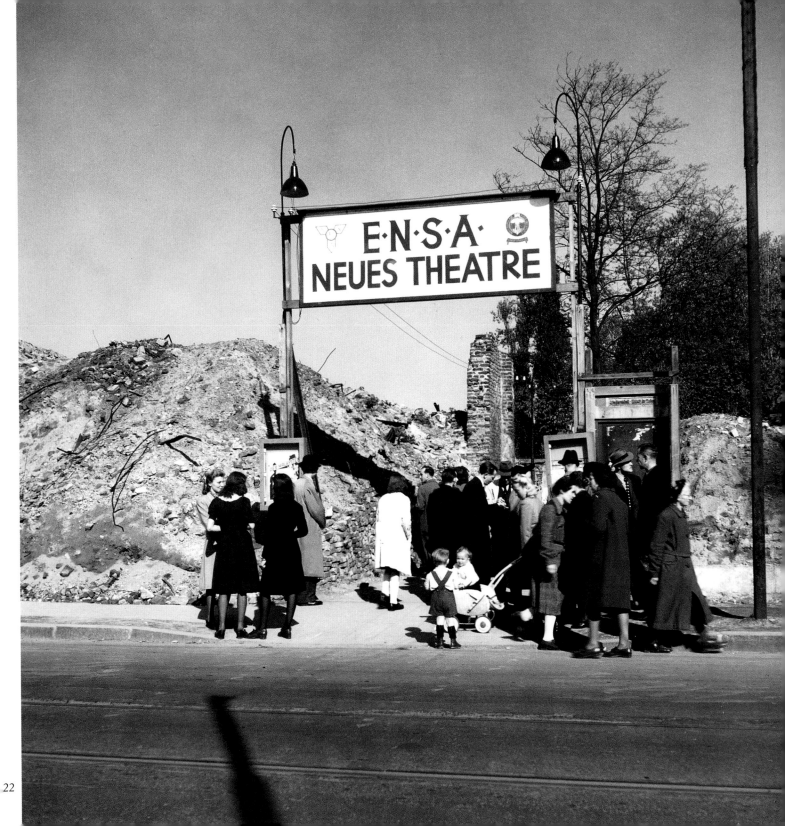

28